Teen ELI Readers A2

The ELI Readers collection is a complete range of books and plays for readers of all ages, ranging from captivating contemporary stories to timeless classics. There are three series, each catering for a different age group; Young ELI Readers, Teen ELI Readers and Young Adult ELI Readers. The books are carefully edited and beautifully illustrated to capture the essence of the stories and plots. The readers are supplemented with 'Focus on' texts packed with background cultural information about the writers and their lives and times.

ANGELA TOMKINSON

LOVING LONDON

ILLUSTRATED BY VERONICA POZZI

Teen ELI Readers

Loving London
by Angela Tomkinson
Language Level Consultants: Janet Borsbey and Ruth Swan
Illustrated by Veronica Pozzi

ELI Readers
Founder and Series Editors
Paola Accattoli, Grazia Ancillani, Daniele Garbuglia (Art Director)

Graphic Design
Airone Comunicazione – Sergio Elisei

Layout
Airone Comunicazione – Sergio Elisei

Production Manager
Francesco Capitano

Photo acknowledgements
© Shutterstock;
© The London Dungeon (courtesy of): pages 12-13;
© Society of London Theatre (courtesy of): pages 26-27;
© Ripley's Believe It or Not (courtesy of): page 31;
© Cartoon Museum (courtesy of): page 31;
© Animals on the Underground (courtesy of): pages 46-47;
© The Great Christmas Pudding Race, S Pakhrin (courtesy of): page 53;
© e-table-interactive (courtesy of): page 55;
© Zoological Society of London: page 57.

P.O. Box 6
62019 Recanati MC
Italy
T +39 071750701
F +39 071977851
info@elionline.com
www.elionline.com

Typeset in 12 / 15 pt Monotype Dante

Printed in Italy by Teconstampa Recanati – ERT.238.01
ISBN 978-88-536-1742-2

First edition: February 2014

www.elireaders.com

Contents

These icons indicate the parts of the story that are recorded

start ▶ **stop** ■

ART

▶ 2 **In London you can find many different types of art – traditional, modern, contemporary, street art and lots more. You can visit one of the many art galleries that London has to offer like the National Gallery or the Tate Modern or just walk around the streets finding some kind of art on every street corner. So let's find out more!**

The front of the Tate Modern

Street Art

Walking round the area of East London you can see the work of more than 40 street artists. Street art includes graffiti and sculpture. Artists use this kind of art to give a message and show how they feel. You can pay to go on a tour with guides who explain the different artwork and what it means. And every time you go back to the area you'll find something new that wasn't there before.

Maid Sweeping by Banksy

Banksy

Around London there is lots of different artwork by the famous British graffiti artist called Banksy. In 2010, Time magazine named him as one of the world's most important people, but nobody knows his real identity*. We never see him in public*, but he always puts his name on his work. His graffiti is sometimes funny and usually has an important message. His work sells for a lot of money.

Pop-Up Art Galleries

In the last few years new kinds of art galleries have arrived in London. They're temporary* galleries that use empty buildings and shops. They are created quickly, stay open for a short time and then close again. Young artists can show their artwork and visitors can buy a painting if they find something they like.

Scary?

Unusual Art Galleries

In London you can also see art in some very unusual places. For example, a cemetery, a public toilet, a platform of Hackney Downs train station in east London, a car park in Peckham in south-east London and the crypt under St Pancras Church in north-west London have all had art shows!

identity: who you are
in public: in the streets
temporary: for a short time

BUILDINGS

3 **Tall buildings, small buildings, historic buildings, modern buildings … you can find them all in London. This is the good thing about this amazing city. No two buildings are the same and there's a big variety of styles and designs. So what's your favourite building in London?**

The Shard ↑
The Gherkin →

London's tallest building

Since 2010 the tallest building in London has been **The Shard.** It's 310 metres tall and has 87 floors. It was designed by the Italian architect Renzo Piano and was finished after three years. It was opened to the public in February 2013 and inside there are offices, a hotel, luxury apartments, shops, restaurants, a spa and a place at the top where you have a wonderful view. On 3rd September 2012, a group of 40 people including Prince Andrew, climbed down from the 87th floor to make money for charity*.

The Gherkin

This is the informal name of a skyscraper* in London's financial district, the City of London. It has this nickname as it is similar to a gherkin*. Although it isn't London's tallest building (it has 41 floors and is 180 metres tall), it is an iconic symbol of the city. You can see it from a distance of 32 kilometres. In September 2006 the building was sold for £630 million. This makes it Britain's most expensive office building!

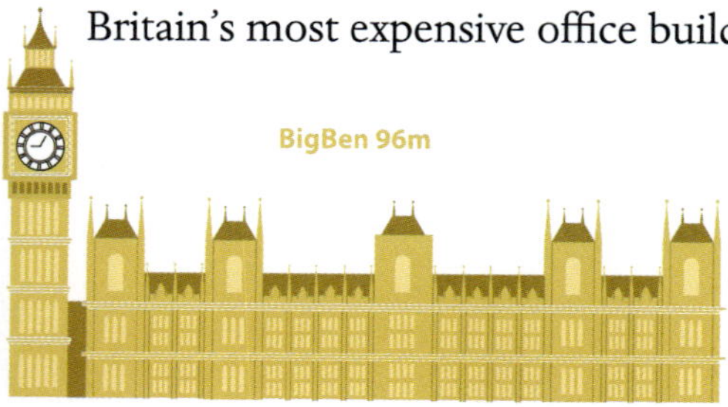

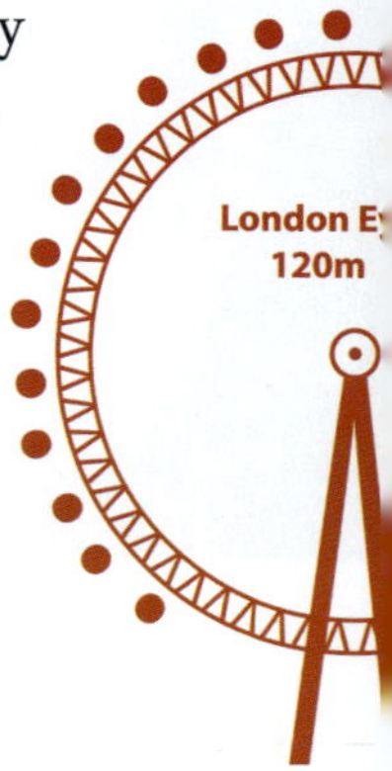

London's smallest building

The smallest house in London is near Marble Arch. It's only a metre wide. It was built in 1805 and only one person, called Lewis Grant Wallace, has ever lived there. Behind the front door there are no rooms on the ground floor. On the first floor there's just a tiny bathroom!

Can you see where it is?

skyscraper: a very tall building
gherkin: a small green vegetable preserved in vinegar
charity: an organisation that gives money to people who need help
fake: not real, false

'Fake' buildings

If you go to this address in London, you'll get a surprise – number 23 and 24 Leinster Gardens, Paddington, London. From the outside they are like two normal houses, but if you look carefully, you'll see they aren't real! The windows and doors are painted on the front of the house – but behind this there's the underground line. The 'fake'* houses are used to cover the underground line behind the buildings.

I think it's a real house but...!

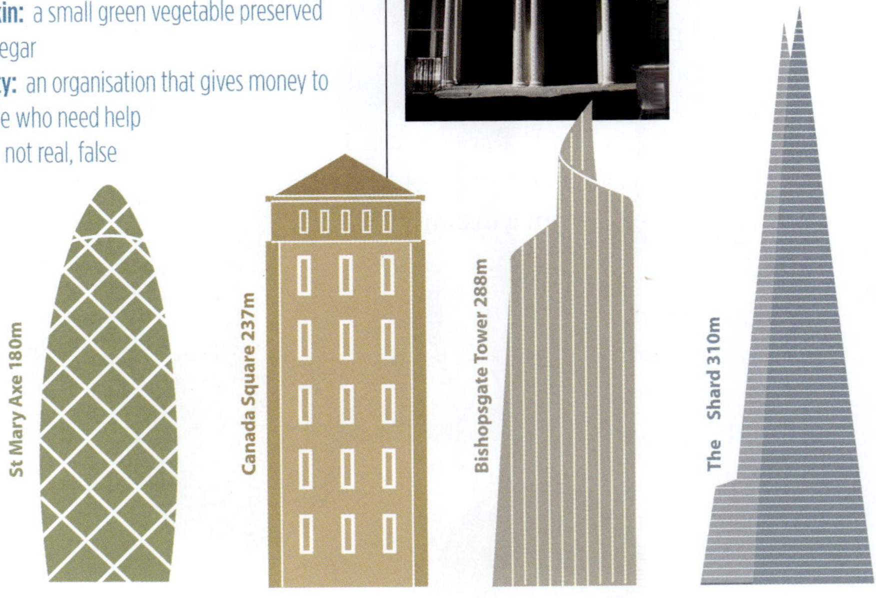

THE CITY

4 **The City is in the heart of London. In the past it was the historic centre of London, but is now the financial and business centre of London. Let's take a tour through the City!**

A City in the City

The area of The City covers only 3 square kilometres, but it's like a real city. It has special political status and also has a police force. The most important person in The City is the Lord Mayor* of the City of London (in fact, London has two mayors, the other is called the Mayor of London).

Banks and Buildings

Here you can find the London Stock Exchange*, the Bank of England, Lloyd's of London and more than 500 other banks. The area is full of skyscrapers and many of London's tallest buildings like the Gherkin are here.

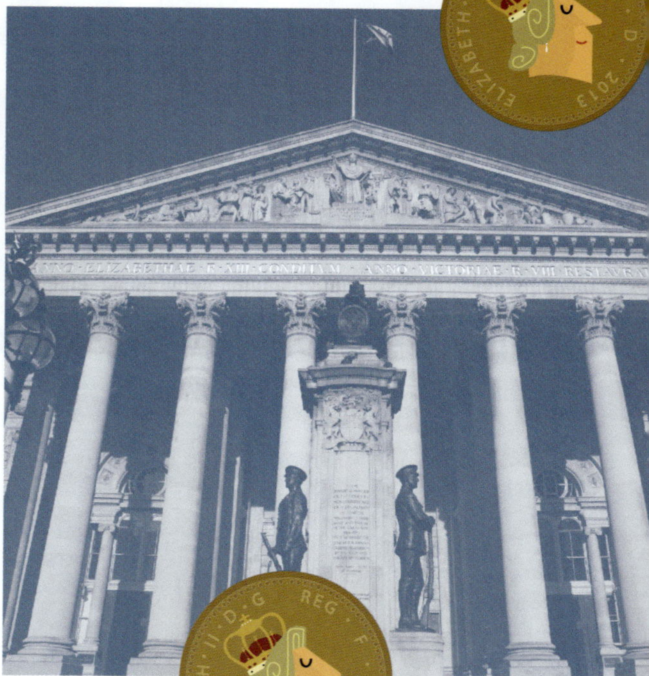

The Bank of England

Culture in the City

The City is also a place of culture. It's home to the London Symphony Orchestra and the Royal Shakespeare Company. An important London monument is found here – St Paul's Cathedral. During the summer months, there's the City of London Festival where visitors can go to concerts and lectures, watch films and go on tours with a guide.

Its nickname

The City is often called **The Square Mile** because the area it covers is 1.12 miles!

St Paul's Cathedral

The Lord Mayor

The Lord Mayor's Show

Every year, there is the Lord Mayor's Show, which is a three-mile long parade for the new Lord Mayor. This tradition has existed since 1215 when King John created a charter* so that the people of London could choose their mayor. The mayor travels the three miles in a carriage made of gold (see picture above) which is used only for the parade once a year. At other times, you can see it inside the Museum of London.

stock exchange: the place where people buy and sell shares in companies
mayor: the most important elected official in a city
a charter: an official document giving rights to the people

THE LONDON DUNGEONS

5 **Do you like being afraid? Do you like knowing about strange things that have happened during history? Then, this is the place for you!**

What is it?

The London Dungeons first opened in London in 1976. It's a museum that shows events from British history. Inside the museum there are characters* and scenes from thousands of years of history like the Great Fire of London of 1666.

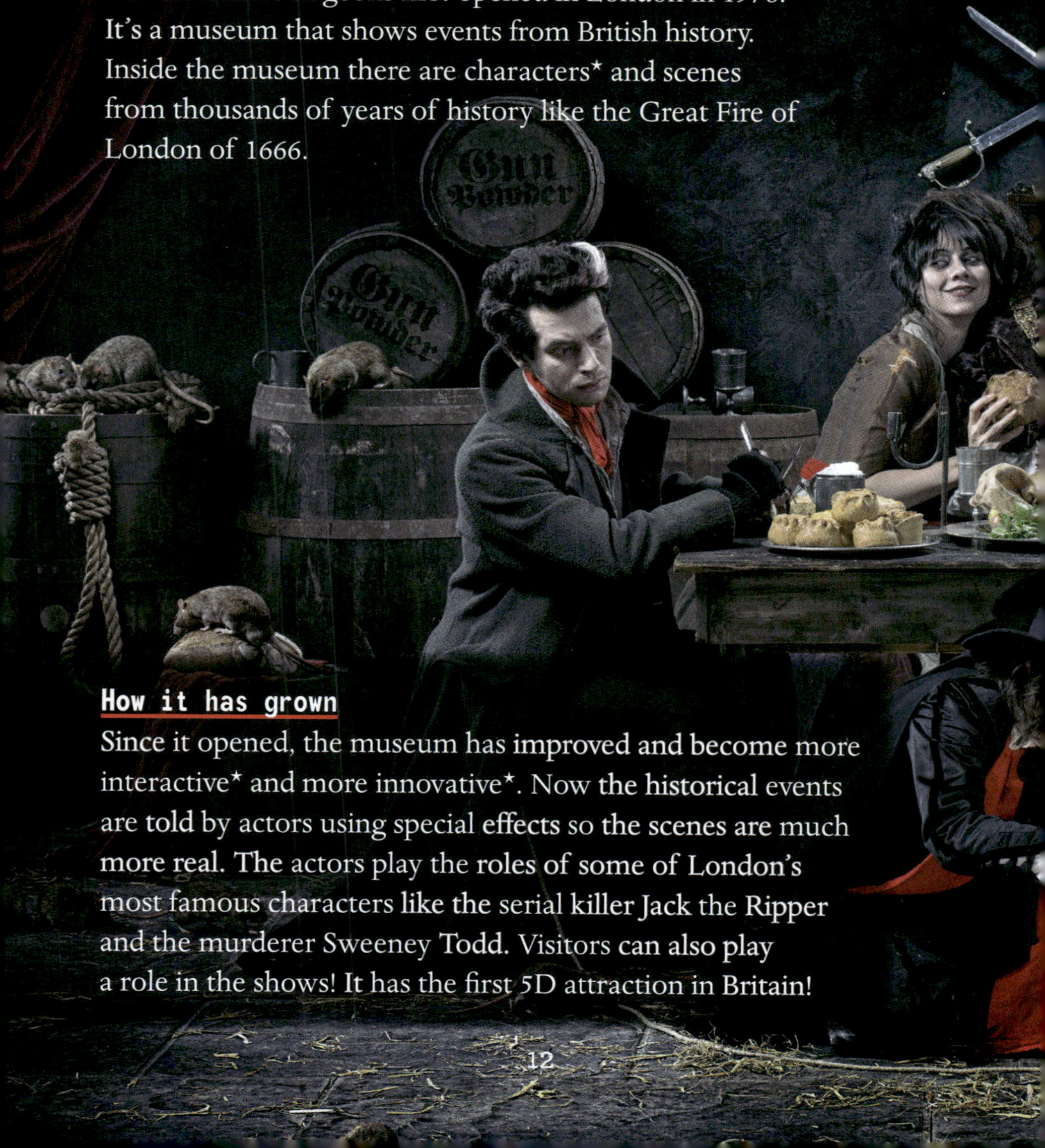

How it has grown

Since it opened, the museum has improved and become more interactive* and more innovative*. Now the historical events are told by actors using special effects so the scenes are much more real. The actors play the roles of some of London's most famous characters like the serial killer Jack the Ripper and the murderer Sweeney Todd. Visitors can also play a role in the shows! It has the first 5D attraction in Britain!

the London Dungeon!

Strange objects to buy

In 2013, the Dungeons changed place from their building near London Bridge to a new building at South Bank, near the London Eye. They didn't need many of the things in the first museum so they decided to organise a kind of market and sell them to the public. Objects like false eyes, false arms and legs and different types of machines were sold!

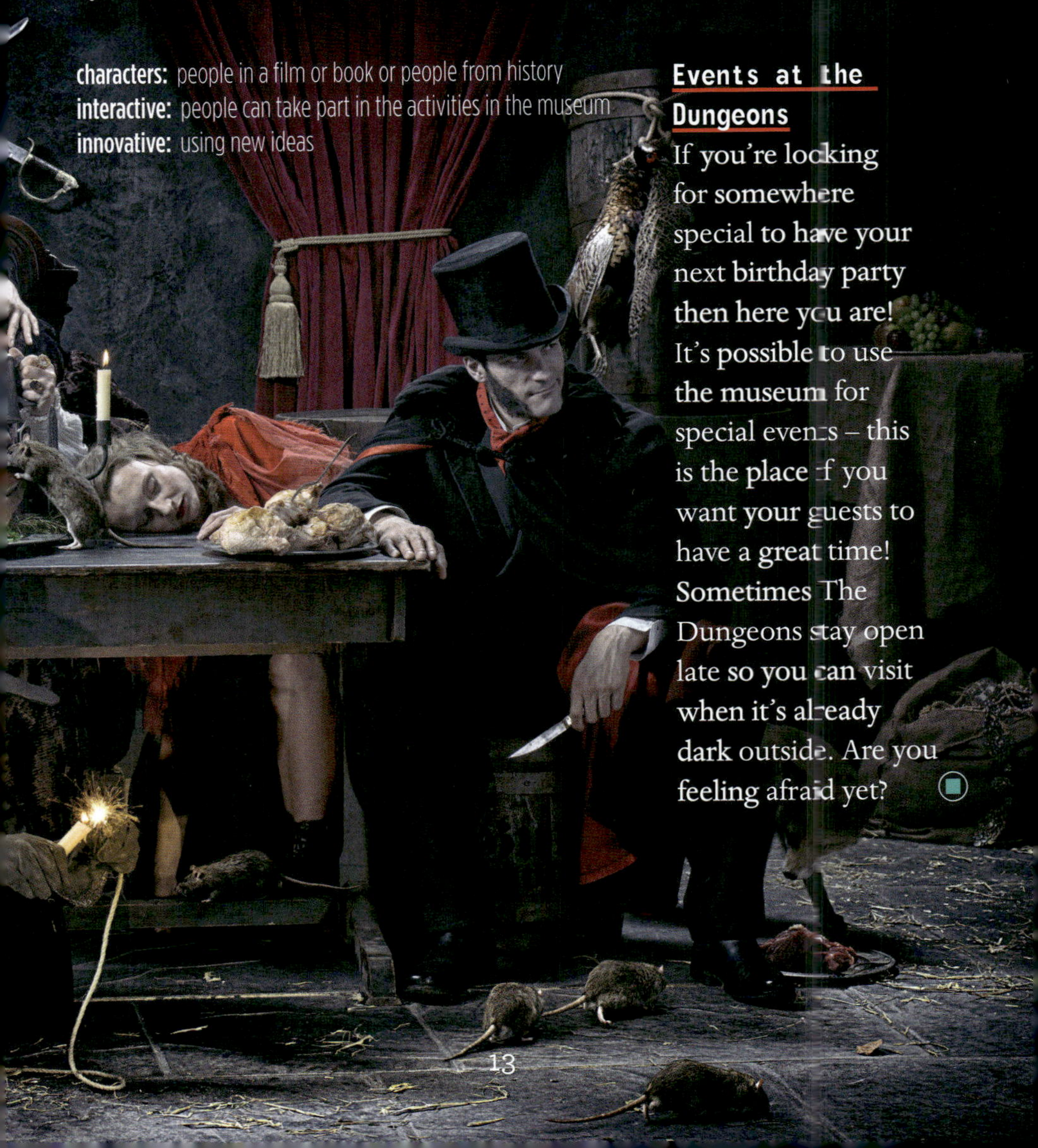

characters: people in a film or book or people from history
interactive: people can take part in the activities in the museum
innovative: using new ideas

Events at the Dungeons

If you're looking for somewhere special to have your next birthday party then here you are! It's possible to use the museum for special events – this is the place if you want your guests to have a great time! Sometimes The Dungeons stay open late so you can visit when it's already dark outside. Are you feeling afraid yet?

EVENTS

6 **London is the capital of fun and there's always something to do. From traditional to modern, exciting events you'll never be bored in this city!**

Everyone loves the carnival

Notting Hill Carnival

The carnival takes place every year in Notting Hill, London. It's on for 3 days in August and has existed for almost 50 years. The West Indian community of London organises the festival and about a million visitors go to watch the event. It's certainly one of the biggest street festivals in the world.
There's music, dancing, food and lots of fun!

Underage Festival

The Underage Festival is a music festival that takes place in Victoria Park in London every August. It's called the Underage Festival as it's for young people from 13 to 17 years old. The organiser of the festival decided to start this event because, when he was 14 years old, he couldn't enter a music concert!

Great Christmas Pudding Race

This unusual event takes place every year at the beginning of December in Covent Garden. All you need is a team of 6 people, a costume and a Christmas pudding, the usual dessert that British people eat at Christmas. You have to run over obstacles while carrying a Christmas Pudding on a plate. This event has existed since 1980, and the money they make from it is for charity.

Dino Snores

Would you like to spend a night sleeping near a big dinosaur? Well, your dream can come true at the National History Museum in London. Once a month, an event is organised in the dinosaur part of the museum where people can spend the night inside. The event starts early evening with various activities about the world of dinosaurs and then at midnight everyone goes to bed! But don't be afraid, if you hear some strange noises during the night … maybe it's only the person next to you who is snoring*!

Would you like to join in the pillow fight?

Pillow* Fight Day

When? April every year. **Where?** Trafalgar Square. **Who?** Anyone can join in. **What mustn't you do?** Don't hit anyone who hasn't got a pillow and don't hit anyone who's using a camera. Do you think it sounds fun? Come along and join in!

Don't snore!

snoring: a noise some people make when they are sleeping
pillow: you put your head on this soft thing in bed

FILMS ABOUT

7 **London is a popular setting* for many films. From classic films like Sherlock Holmes, and ones based on the books of Charles Dickens, to romantic comedies like Bridget Jones's Diary and Notting Hill. Let's look at some of the more modern ones.**

The aliens are here!

Alex in London

Attack the Block

If you like films about aliens and monsters, then this is the film for you! The film was made in 2011 and the setting is South London. It's about a teenage street gang who meets aliens who want to attack London. The popular British electronic dance music group *Basement Jaxx* made the music on the film's soundtrack*.

Stormbreaker

This is the film of the first book in the Alex Rider series which was written by Anthony Horowitz. Alex Rider is a 15-year old spy who goes to work for the British Secret Service after his uncle is killed. In the film, places in London like Hyde Park, Piccadilly Circus and the Science Museum are shown. In the film there are different action scenes like a horse chase* through the centre of London and a fight on top of a London skyscraper.

Can you name them?

My name's Bond ... James Bond!

James Bond

In the James Bond film of 2012, *Skyfall*, a variety of London places were used. Some scenes were filmed in different underground stations, the National Gallery, Charing Cross Station, the Old Royal Naval College in Greenwich, Tower Hill and Parliament Square. Some of the film was also set and filmed in China. However, some London settings were also used but they were changed to be like China. For example, the entrance to London's 4th tallest building was used and it was covered with lights to be like Shanghai!

setting: the time and place of the film
soundtrack: music from a film
chase: follow someone quickly

Harry Potter

In the Harry Potter series of films you can see some famous places in London like London Zoo, Piccadilly Circus, King's Cross Station, St Pancras Station, Millennium Bridge, Charing Cross Road in London's West End and Westminster tube station. In some of the films, there is Diagon Alley, which is a shopping street in London where the wizards go to buy the things they need to do their magic.

GREENWICH

ROYAL
OBSERVATORY
GREENWICH

8 One very important area in London that is rich in history is Greenwich. It's in south-east London and it's now a UNESCO World Heritage Site*. But do you know what it's famous for? Read on to find out!

The Prime Meridian Line

What time is it?

Most people know Greenwich, as it was here, in 1884, that Greenwich Mean Time (GMT) was born. At the beginning it was used to speak about the time at the Royal Observatory in Greenwich, but then it became a time standard all over the world. World time zones use this reference and different countries are a certain number of hours in front of or behind GMT. So what time zone is your country in?

The Prime Meridian

In Greenwich you can also find the Prime Meridian. This is a vertical line that marks the zero degree longitude measurement on Earth. It goes from the North Pole to the South Pole through Greenwich. It divides the Earth's surface into the Eastern and Western Hemisphere.

Royal Greenwich

In the 15th century a royal palace was built in Greenwich, called the Palace of Placentia. Kings and Queens like Henry VIII and Elizabeth I were born there. Many centuries later, in 2012, Queen Elizabeth II gave Greenwich the status of 'Royal Borough' for the first time in more than 80 years (there are four other royal boroughs* in London). This was because there has been a strong link between Greenwich and the royal family since medieval times.

What time is it, please?

The Cutty Sark

Greenwich and the sea

Greenwich also has important links with the sea. It's home to the National Maritime museum, the world's largest maritime museum. The Old Royal Naval college, designed by Sir Christopher Wren, and the Cutty Sark, a 19th century sailing ship that transported tea from China, are also here. They're all open to visitors and you can spend an exciting day looking at these things of historical importance.

The first shop in the world

A shop named Nauticalia, which sells maritime objects, is the first shop in the world because it's at 4/10 of a minute west of the Meridian Line!

World Heritage Site: a title given to places of historical importance
boroughs: administrative areas inside a city

HARRODS

9 **One of the icons of shopping in London is the famous department store, Harrods. You can't visit London without going to this luxurious, elegant shopping paradise!**

Where it all started

Harrods started as a grocery* in the East End of London in 1834. The owner was Charles Harrod and he sold tea. After some years, he decided to move to a 'nicer, cleaner' area, so he bought a place in Knightsbridge. This is where Harrods is still today. The new shop began in only one room but grew very fast and by 1880, 100 people were working there.

From disaster to success

Unfortunately, in 1883 there was a very big fire and the store was destroyed. However, the owner didn't lose hope and he built the store again. At this time, Harrods had many famous customers like the writer Oscar Wilde, the psychoanalyst Sigmund Freud and many members of the British Royal Family.

The first moving stairs

In 1898, the first escalator* in the world was put inside Harrods. Customers didn't usually move so fast to go upstairs, so nervous customers were given something to drink when they arrived at the top to help them feel better!

The world's first escalator!

From Knightsbridge to Egypt

In 1985, Mohammed Al-Fayed became the owner of Harrods. He was the father of Dodi Al-Fayed, who was killed in a car crash in Paris in 1997 with Princess Diana. There are two memorials* inside the store to remember them. However, in 2010, he decided to stop work and the famous store now belongs to some Arab businessmen.

Does anyone want to buy a lion?

Animals and Harrods

The store doesn't only sell clothes, food and jewellery but also animals! Some years ago it sold a baby elephant called Gertie that was a present for the US President Reagan. Another time the store bought a baby lion from a zoo. One night, the lion got out of its cage and destroyed the Harrods carpet department! Later, the lion was bought by two Australians who let it live free in Africa.

grocery: a small shop selling food and things for the home
escalator: (see picture on page 20)
memorial: a monument to remember someone

ICONS

10 **What do you think of when you hear the word London? Many symbols of London life come to mind*. Here are just a few of them.**

Red double-decker buses

Everyone is familiar with these iconic symbols of London but not many people know they're really called Routemasters. These are the usual buses with two floors that were open at the back so people could jump on and off them when the bus stopped. They were first used in 1956 and were regularly used until 2005. However, a new design was made in 2012 just in time for the 2012 London Olympics!

Who's calling?

Jump on ... jump off!

Red phone boxes

The first red phone box was invented by Sir Giles Gilbert Scott in 1924. He won a competition which was organised by the London council to design a phone box! The design has changed since the first one and now there are very few on the streets. 'In 2012 the British telephone company, British telecom, for the 25th anniversary of the free phone charity 'Childline', asked 80 different artists to design and decorate different phone boxes. They were put around London and then later sold at an auction*.

How well do you know the streets of London?

Black taxi cabs

While New York has its famous yellow taxis, London has its own icon – the black hackney cab. They are called a hackney or hackney carriage. They were introduced in the late 1950s and today you can find them in all different colours, but at the beginning they were black. Drivers of these taxis have to pass a difficult test called 'the knowledge' to have a licence*. They have to know the streets and buildings of London perfectly. A black hackney was used in the 2012 London Olympics closing ceremony – it transported the Spice Girls onto the stage!

Phew ... t's hot under here!

Beefeaters

These are the guards that are found at the Tower of London, also known as Yeoman Warders. They were first introduced by King Henry VII in 1485. Their job was to look after prisoners in the tower and guard the Crown Jewels. Now, they are more like tour guides answering tourists' questions and are also a visitor attraction.

come to mind: come into your head
auction: a place where things are sold to the person who offers the most money
licence: a document that shows you can do something

THE CROWN JEWELS

11 **Jewels, jewels and more jewels! The collection of the Crown Jewels, in the Tower of London, is one of the most priceless* collections in the world. Let's learn something about these wonderful things!**

Queen Elizabeth II

Accessories

So what does a king or queen usually use for important royal events? In the crown jewel collection you can find crowns, sceptres, orbs, swords, rings and spurs* (see pictures on page 61). Something for every moment! And we can say that the British Royal Family is the only monarchy in Europe that still uses its crown jewels when a new king or queen comes to the throne*!

Not the real ones

The jewels that you can see in the Tower are a copy of the original ones. During the English Civil War, when England became a republic for 11 years, the jewels were destroyed by Oliver Cromwell and his men. However, when the monarchy returned in 1660, the jewels were made again.

Jewels

There are many famous gem* stones in the collection, but probably the most famous is the First Star of Africa. It's on the royal sceptre and is the largest diamond without any colour in the world. It weighs 530 carats (110 grams)! The sceptre was originally made when King Charles II became king in 1661.

Stolen jewels

In 1671, a man called Colonel Blood tried to steal the jewels. He was caught a short time after. Fortunately for him, the king forgave him and gave him some land in Ireland!

The guards

The jewels are well looked after inside the tower by the Yeoman Warders, or Beefeaters as they're also known. In 1485, King Henry VII started this tradition and they have looked after the jewels since then.

priceless: (here) too expensive to buy today
spurs: a metal object on the heel of a rider's boot
throne: a special chair that a king or queen sits on
gem: a diamond or another expensive stone

KIDSWEEK

12

Would you like to go to the theatre? Then this important event that happens once a year is for you! Let's find out more!

What it is

Kidsweek takes place every summer in London's theatre district, the West End. It's famous for its big number of theatres (about 50) and millions of theatre-lovers and tourists go to see a West End show every year. Thanks to *Kidsweek*, children under 16 can see lots of shows for free and take part in fun workshops with the stars.

Shows

Some of the shows that kids can join in, are well-loved classics like *The Lion King*, *Charlie and the Chocolate Factory* and *Shrek the Musical*. One of the most popular shows is *Matilda the Musical*. It's based on the children's book by Roald Dahl and tells the story of 5-year old Matilda, very intelligent for her age, who goes away to school and finds that it's very different from what she thought!

The West End

It's also known as 'Theatreland' because it has a lot of theatres. It's quite normal for West End shows to run* for many years and Agatha Christie's murder mystery play *The Mousetrap* has been on at the theatre in London since 1952. It's the world's longest running show! The West End is also famous for its musicals – plays with lots of songs – and the longest running musical in the West End is *Les Miserables*. It's been on at the theatre in London since 1985.

Do you want to act?

London is also home to the National Youth Theatre that helps children and teenagers to make their dream of acting come true. Many famous British actors like Orlando Bloom, Colin Firth, Jude Law, Daniel Craig and Daniel Day-Lewis started acting in this youth group when they were children. And look where they are today!

Higher ... higher!

run: be acted in the theatre

LANDMARKS

13 **A landmark is a famous building or monument that you can see and understand very easily what it is. In London there are hundreds to choose from so let's take a look!**

A London landmark on the river

A suspension bridge

An important London landmark is Tower Bridge. It's a bridge with two towers joined by two walkways and it opens for boats to pass through. Today, the bridge opens much less than in the past and you have to ask to open it 24 hours before you need to pass through. However, in December 2012, the bridge had to open very quickly as a 15 metre rubber duck was moving down the River Thames! Many people couldn't believe their eyes, but it was a marketing event to give money to people who had good ideas to make people laugh!

Is it a clock, a tower or …..?

If you ask people to name the most famous landmark in London, they probably say Big Ben. But did you know that Ben Ben isn't the name of the famous clock or tower that you see in many films or photos about London? It's the name of the bell inside the clock tower! And the clock tower is now called the 'Elizabeth Tower'. It was changed for Queen Elizabeth II's Diamond Jubilee* in 2012. And did you know that the tower isn't straight? Every year it moves by 0.9 millimetres.

A modern-day landmark

It stands on the bank of the River Thames, is 135 metres tall, moves 26 cm per second and you can see for 40 kilometres from it. Can you guess what it is? Yes, it's the London Eye, Europe's tallest panoramic wheel. It was built for the Millennium in 2000 and has become one of the most popular tourist attractions in London. On New Year's Eve every year, there are fireworks near the wheel and for Prince William and Kate Middleton's wedding* in 2012, the wheel was covered with lights with the colours of the Union Jack flag – red, white and blue.

London's biggest square

Trafalgar Square was built in 1845 to remember the Battle of Trafalgar in 1805. Every year, thousands of people go to Trafalgar Square on New Year's Eve to wait for midnight. In July 2011, the square was used for the first time for the world premiere of the final film in the Harry potter series *The Deathly Hallows – Part 2.*

Diamond Jubilee: when a king or queen has been on the throne for sixty years
wedding: when two people get married

London with many lights

The famous fountain in Trafalgar Square

MUSEUMS

14 **London is home to more than 240 museums and there are museums for everybody! You can spend days walking around the Natural History Museum, the Science Museum, the British Museum, the Victoria and Albert Museum … and still not see everything. But let's take a look at some of the more unusual museums that London has to offer.**

Elementary, my dear Watson

Everyone knows the famous detective Sherlock Holmes stories, written by the author Sir Arthur Conan Doyle. Well, it says in the stories that Sherlock lived at 221b Baker Street in London between 1881 and 1904 and this is where you can find the Sherlock Holmes Museum. You can visit Sherlock's study where all his personal belongings* are in their usual place like his famous hat, his pipe and his magnifying glass (see the picture below). You can even sit in his armchair near the fire and try to find the answer to the crime!

Playing detectives

And if visiting the Sherlock Holmes Museum isn't enough for you and you want more, there's the Crime Museum, also called the Black Museum. It's at New Scotland Yard, home of the London Police Force. It was started in 1874 to help the police study crime and criminals*. There are two parts to the museum. The first is a copy of the original museum, while the second has many things from 20th century crimes.

Believe it or not!

In Piccadilly Circus, in the centre of London, you can find a very unusual museum. It's called 'Ripley's Believe it or Not' and it has more than 700 very strange objects. These were all collected by Robert Ripley, who was a reporter and a cartoonist, on his travels around the world during the 1920s and 1930s.

Cartoons

In 2006, London's first cartoon museum opened. It's near the British Museum and has many examples of cartoons and comic art from the 18th century to today. It has a collection of more than 1,700 original cartoons and pictures. Every year there are the *Young Cartoonist of the Year* awards.

Unusual faces!

Anyone for a drink?

belongings: the things that people have got
criminals: people who steal or kill or do other wrong things

NATURE

▶ 15 **London is a big city, a sort of 'urban jungle', but it's still home to a big variety of wildlife, including many protected species. There are a large number of nature reserves inside the city and you can find wildlife where you don't expect it!**

A hidden paradise

Not many people know, but behind King's Cross Station, there's a hidden* paradise. It's Camley Street Natural Park. You can go there to be far from the noise and chaos of the city. There are a lot of trees, a pond* and a large variety of plants and animals. Many community events happen there and there's an education programme for school children who can go there and learn about nature.

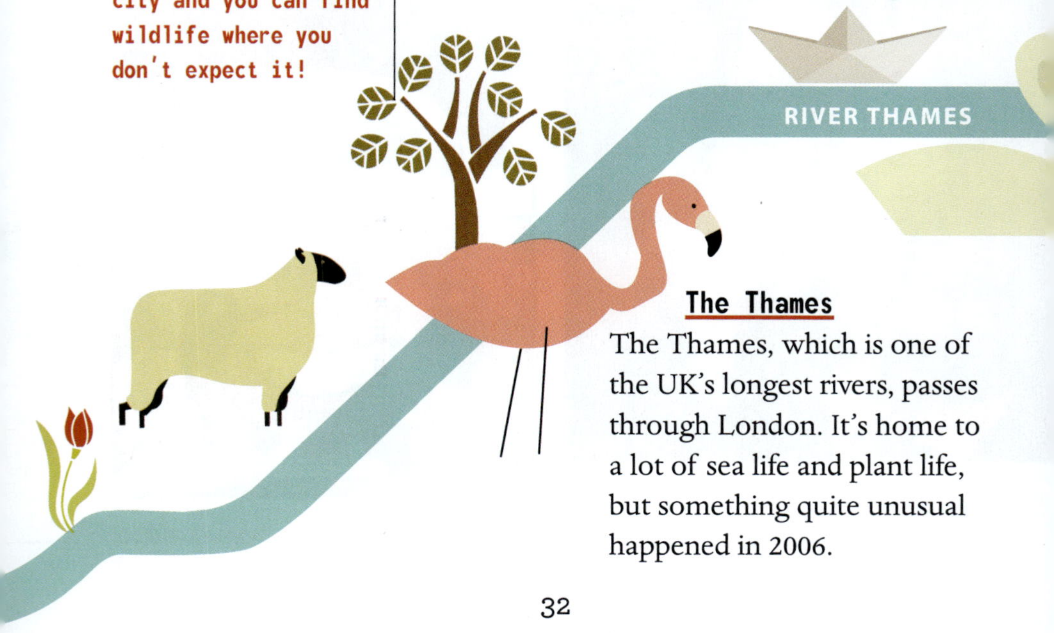

The Thames

The Thames, which is one of the UK's longest rivers, passes through London. It's home to a lot of sea life and plant life, but something quite unusual happened in 2006.

A free ride

And if you decide to take the underground in London, don't be surprised if you see some 'passengers' without a ticket! It's quite normal for pigeons to enter the carriages when the doors are open and take a ride on the underground for free. But passengers were very surprised when a fox got on at one of the stops and sat down some years ago!

A bird on the underground

Plant a tree

In May 2013 London's first ever *Tree Week* happened. It was decided by the Mayor of London who has promised to make the city greener. It's going to happen every year and there are workshops, exhibitions, guided walking tours, and people can help plant thousands of new trees in the city.

hidden: something that's not easy to see or find
pond: a small lake

A large whale was seen swimming in the river in the centre of London. This was a new experience for London, and lots of people tried to save the whale. Unfortunately, this wasn't possible and its skeleton was given to the Natural History Museum for scientific study.

OUTSIDE LONDON

▶ 16 **It's impossible to be bored in London – there are so many things happening and so many things to see. However, places near London also offer a lot of interest, history and culture. Are you ready to go?**

Windsor

It's home to the biggest and oldest castle (where people still live) in the world! It's used by the Queen at weekends and for some royal events. It was built in the 11th century and has seen bombs during the war and a big fire. In Windsor, you can also find 'Legoland', a theme park made of the popular building blocks Lego. All the attractions are built with Lego!

Windsor Castle

Hampton Court

Hampton Court Palace

This royal palace, in Richmond upon Thames, belonged to King Henry VIII. The people who look after the palace say they have seen the ghost of the king inside the palace. People also say that there are the ghosts of two of Henry's ex wives, Jane Seymour and Catherine Howard.

The palace is also famous for its maze* that was built in 1690. It's a very long maze and it's very easy to get lost inside!

Go Ape

If you like climbing around, then this is the place for you. It's an outdoor adventure course using trees. It takes place in the forest using rope ladders*, rope bridges and swings. You can swing, climb and slide as much as you like. However, it isn't for everybody – you have to be more than 10 years old, not be too short and wear a safety harness (see picture on the right) at all times!

Chessington World of Adventure

This is a theme park, zoo and sea life centre 20 kilometres from London. It has more than 1,000 animals and you can see many of them from the train that goes around the park.

There are 10 different areas in the adventure park each with a different theme like Transylvania, the Forbidden Kingdom and the Pirate's Cove. There's also the Madagascar Live Show which has all the characters from the children's film.

maze: you get lost in a maze and you have to find the way out

ladders: a moveable structure that helps you go up and down

PEOPLE

▶ 17 **In London there are about 7 million people. It's a multi-cultural city where more than 300 languages are spoken. So let's find out about some of the people who live and work here.**

Cockneys

A Cockney is a person who was born in the East End of London. People say that if you were born near St Mary-le-Bow Church and you can hear the church bells ringing then you're a Cockney. Cockneys have their own language, where all the words rhyme (have the same sound) but are very different from the word they are talking about. Some examples are: apples and pears = stairs, dog and bone = phone, Jack Jones = alone.

Pearly Kings and Queens

In 1875, a man called Henry Croft started putting buttons on his clothes to make people notice* him and to make money for charity. The 'fashion' became popular with street sellers and working class people. The clothes that this group of people wear, use as many as 30,000 buttons and are sometimes heavier than 30 kilos. The clothes are passed from generation to generation and they are worn at charity events, weddings and other family festivals.

A world in one city

London is home to a big variety of ethnic groups* and 37% of the population of London was born outside Britain. The biggest ethnic group in London is people from Asia and there are many Indians and Bangladeshis. The next biggest group is Africans coming from Africa but also the Caribbean, for example Jamaica. The Chinese also play an important part in London life and you can visit the Chinese area of the city called 'Chinatown' to eat in one of the many Chinese restaurants there.

Everyone is in a hurry!

Commuters

This large group of people also plays an important part in the life of the city. They are the people who live outside the city but travel into the city every day for work. They usually live in the small towns and villages in the areas outside the city. Commuters to London spend five weeks a year getting to work and back!

notice: look at
ethnic groups: groups of people who have the same culture and traditions

THE QUEEN

18 **One of the most important symbols of London is the Queen. She's been on the throne since 1953 and has been the Queen for a very long time! Read on to find out more!**

Smile Philip! They're taking our photograph!

ID card
Name: Elizabeth Alexandra Mary Windsor
Born: 21st April, 1926
Address: Buckingham Palace, London SW1A 1AA
Family: Married to Prince Philip. They have 4 children (Anne, Charles, Andrew, Edward) and 8 grandchildren
Hobbies: Horses, walking with her dogs and Scottish country dancing

A normal day in the life of the Queen

It isn't easy being the Queen! She has many different duties* to do each day, both in private and in public. Some of her jobs are meetings with heads of state, dinner parties and visits inside the UK and to other countries. She also does many other jobs like reading and answering letters from the public (she receives around 200-300 letters every day) reading and signing official documents, meetings with her secretaries to talk about what's planned for the day and meetings with political ministers or ambassadors.

God save the Queen!

Etiquette*

If you ever meet the Queen, you should call her 'Your Majesty' and never only 'you'. Women should give a little curtsy* and only shake her hand if she gives you her hand first. You should follow a dress code – usually formal clothes, and stand up when the Queen enters the room. And of course, if you're invited to dinner, you shouldn't start eating until the Queen starts!

Did you know…?

The Queen has two birthdays a year! Her 'real' birthday is 21st April, the day she was born, while her 'official' birthday is in June. The Queen usually spends her 'real' birthday in private with her family, but every year at 12 o'clock, 41 guns are fired by the royal guards to wish her a happy birthday. However, during her 'official' birthday there is the Trooping of the Colours. It's a big military parade that takes place in the centre of London.

duties: jobs, things you have to do
etiquette: what you have to do in important social situations
curtsy: when a woman bends her knees to say hello to a king or queen

RECREATION

19

How much is this?

So how do Londoners spend their free time in the city? There are so many things to choose from! There are always things happening not only for the tourists that visit the city, but also for the people who live and work in the capital.

Shall we buy this?

Just Looking

London is famous for its markets. There are hundreds to choose from and they sell all different kinds of things – clothes, antiques*, food, furniture, books, flowers, vintage and lots more. You can spend hours just walking around them looking for something to buy. Many tourists also visit some of the famous markets, for example, Camden Market, Portobello Market, Brick Lane Market and Petticoat Lane Market.

Car boot sales

In some areas of the city, car boot* sales are organised. People take their old things to sell and put little tables next to their cars. If you want to sell at one of these car boot sales, you usually have to pay a little money. That isn't a problem; people love car boot sales, so you can make a lot of money selling things. They usually start early in the morning, so if you want to sell, you have to get up very early!

A strange place to have a coffee?

Would you like a coffee?

Londoners love going to coffee shops and more people drink coffee now than the traditional tea. In London you can find the usual coffee shops that are all over the UK, but also some very unusual places to drink your coffee. For example, would you like to have a coffee inside a Victorian public toilet or in a bicycle repair shop? No problem! Or how about inside the crypt of a church near Charing Cross?

Parks and more parks

When the sun comes out, many Londoners visit one of the green areas inside the city. Some of the more popular parks are Hyde Park, Regent's Park, St James's Park, Richmond Park, Clapham Common and Hampstead Heath. People go there to walk their dogs, sunbathe*, jog or go for a walk and leave the noise and chaos of the city behind.

antiques: very old things
car boot: the back of the car where you put things
sunbathe: sit or lie in the sun

SPORT

20 **What's your favourite sport? If it's football, tennis, rugby, cricket or other sports, you'll find something for you in London!**

Goal!

The most popular sport in London is football. The city is home to 14 professional football clubs and they're usually named after the area in London in which they play. London's oldest football club is Fulham and its most successful teams are probably Arsenal, Chelsea and Tottenham Hotspur. London is also home to Wembley Stadium, England's national stadium, where important cup finals and international matches are played.

Watching a match at Wimbledon

Anyone for tennis?

Wimbledon is the oldest tennis competition in the world and was first played in 1877. It takes place in London in June. It's the only important tennis competition still played on grass. During the matches, the players can only wear white and not any other colour! It's also traditional to eat strawberries and cream at Wimbledon.

An oval ball

The game of rugby is also very popular in London and the city is home to 13 rugby teams that play in national leagues*. Some of the most famous London teams are the London Wasps, Harlequins and Saracens. Twickenham Stadium, where the English rugby team plays their matches, is in South London. It's the biggest rugby stadium in the world and the 2nd largest stadium in the UK after Wembley.

The famous boat race

Every year on the River Thames in London there's the Oxford and Cambridge Boat Race. It's a race between the two universities. The first race was in 1829. Cambridge have won more races than Oxford but things can change very quickly!

leagues: a group of teams who often play matches against each other

TRADITIONS

21 **In London there are many different customs and traditions and visitors love them all. For example, you can't visit London without going to Buckingham Palace to see the Changing of the Guards. Let's look at some other traditions that London has to offer.**

Say what you think

Speakers' Corner is in Hyde Park. It's an area where people can say what they think and discuss their opinion with others outside in the park. Anyone can speak but only if what they want to say doesn't hurt other people. This tradition started in 1866 and some famous visitors to the corner have been the German philosopher and economist Karl Marx, the writer George Orwell and the Russian leader Lenin.

Speaking in Hyde Park

Would you like a cuppa*?

The Ritz in London is one of the finest hotels in the world. One of its traditions is afternoon tea: people can choose from 17 different types of tea and various types of cake. And, why not try a cucumber sandwich? To go there for afternoon tea you have to wear formal dress (no jeans or trainers) and you need to book a table about 12 weeks before you want to go!

tea TIME

Running with a pancake

Twelfth Night

Twelfth Night

An event that happens every year in the Bankside area of London is Twelfth Night. It's on the evening of January 5th and is at the end of the twelve days of Christmas. At Bankside Twelfth Night, a group of actors do a play that comes from the past. Special cakes are given to the people who are watching. Inside two of the cakes is a bean and a pea. If you find the bean, you become King Bean and if you find the pea, you become Queen Pea. Then everyone walks around .... with King Bean and Queen Pea at the front.

Pancake race

On Shrove Tuesday, the day before Ash Wednesday and the first day of Lent*, people usually eat pancakes in the UK. In London you'll find the Great Spitalfields Pancake Race on this day. At the beginning it was in Covent Garden, then Soho and now it's near Brick Lane. Teams of four people wearing costumes run up and down while throwing a pancake in the air and catching it. The money made from this event goes to charity.

cuppa: a cup of tea
Lent: the period of 40 days before Easter

THE UNDERGROUND

▶ 22 You can't visit London without a trip on this important symbol of London, also known as the 'Tube'. Do you want to know more? Then read below!

Some numbers

The underground started working in 1863. It has 11 different lines, 270 stations and 402 kilometres of track. Around 3.5 million people use it every day and it's the world's fourth largest underground network.

The map of the underground, which was designed by Harry Beck in 1931, is an icon of design. You can find the design on t-shirts, mugs*, posters, mouse mats and even mobile phone cases.

Which animals can you see?

Animals on the underground

People use Harry Beck's map to help them travel around the underground network, but did you know that inside the map, there's a world of animals made by using the tube lines and stations on the map! The animals were found by Paul Middlewick, an artist, in 1988. One day, while he was travelling home from work, he was looking at the tube map and he saw the body of an elephant. As well as the elephant, he has found many others – around 38 animals! Which ones can you see on the map?

No trousers day

If you're travelling on the tube on a very cold day in January, don't be surprised if you see lots of people wearing coats, hats and gloves but without trousers, only in their underwear! It's a kind of flash mobbing* that started in New York in 2002 and has moved to other cities. The idea behind this event is to make 'scenes of chaos and happiness in public places'.

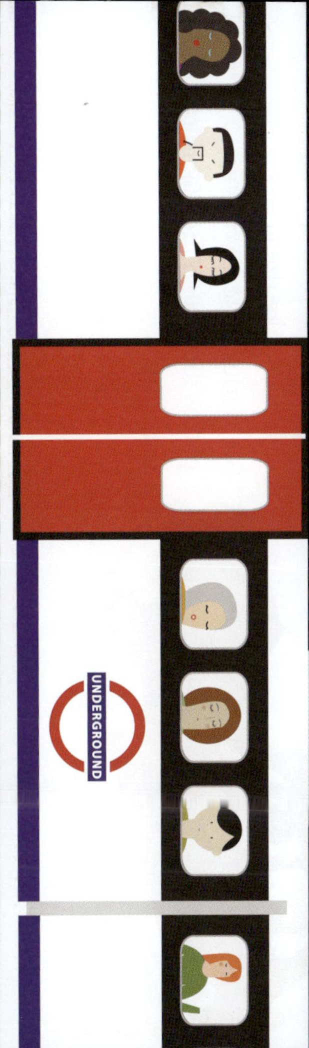

Happy birthday to you!

Happy Birthday

In 2013, the London Underground had its 150th anniversary. There were a lot of events, like an exhibition of posters showing the tube from the 19th century to today and a London Underground afternoon tea, with sandwiches and cakes made to show different underground stations. Here's to another 150 years!

mugs: cups

flash mobbing: a group of people who suddenly get together in a public place, perform an unusual activity and then move on

VEHICLES

23 **If you think travelling round London by underground or double-decker bus is boring, then why not try some of the more unusual ways to travel round the city? Take a look!**

Kayaking down the Thames

Canoeing

If you're feeling full of energy and want to do exercise while you visit London, then this is the one for you. You can go on a kayak tour (see the photo) on the river but also the many canals that London has. The city has more than 160 kilometres of water so you'll always have somewhere to go in your kayak.

By water? Or by road?

By duck

If you can't decide if you prefer travelling by road or water then this is the vehicle for you! It's an amphibious vehicle that travels both on water and on land. It's bright yellow in colour so you can't miss it! Duck Tours. You can visit the most important places in London, or go on a special tour, like the James Bond tour, where you visit places that are in the 007 books and films.

Jump on the boat

Thames Clippers are a kind of water bus on the river. Many commuters use them to get to work, but tourists also use them to visit the places along the river. Around 7,500 passengers travel on these boats every day. If you're interested in art, you can use the 'Tate to Tate' boat which takes you from the Tate Modern gallery to the Tate Britain on the other side of the river.

A nice way to go to work

Trains with no driver

The Docklands Light Railway started in 1987. It takes passengers to the Docklands area of the city in East London. This area was developed* in the 1980s and is now an important financial and commercial area. The train is automatic, which means that there are no drivers on the train. It works from a central control point.

Where's the driver?

Back to the 1960s

If you like British cars and 1960s music, then why not go on a tour of London by Mini Cooper? A driver will take you around London in the car and he'll explain about the places you see on the tour in a very funny and interesting way. And you can listen to some 1960s music on the car's MP3 player. ■

A 'mini' tour

developed: improved, made better

WRITERS

24 Many well-known writers were born in London and call London their home. The city has an important role in some of their works and it has given them a lot of ideas for their writing. Let's take a look at some of them!

Zadie Smith - A picture of London

Zadie Smith is probably one of London's most well-known modern writers. She was born in London in 1975 to a Jamaican mother and British father. She has written four very successful books and has won various prizes for her writing. Her novel, *NW*, is set in a poor area of North-West London and is about four young people who grew up there.

Sophie Kinsella - I love shopping

Sophie Kinsella is from London too and is a well-known writer of 'chick lit' (books that are funny and not serious, usually written for girls). Her most popular books have been about Becky Bloomwood, a shopaholic* who can't stop shopping. The first two books are also films, and show how Becky's love for shopping makes her life very difficult.

Zadie Smith

Sophie Kinsella

Monica Ali - From Bangladesh to London

Monica Ali is half Bangladeshi and half British, but she grew up in London. Her first book, *Brick Lane*, was nominated* for an important literary prize and was also made into a film. The book takes its name from the well-known street in London, Brick Lane, which is where many of London's Bangladeshi people live. The book speaks about a young Bangladeshi woman that moves to London to marry an older man and tells the story of her life in this new country.

shopaholic: someone who can't stop shopping
nominated: say that someone should win an important prize

Charlie Higson - Zombies everywhere

Charlie Higson has written many books in his life and he's well-known for his Young Bond series of James Bond books for younger readers. His new series of books, *The Enemy* (2009), *The Dead* (2010), *The Fear* (2011) and *The Sacrifice* (2012) are all set in London. The books are about a virus that changes adults into zombies. So it's the children that have to find the answer to this big problem.

Monica Ali

Charlie Higson

25 **Xmas (Christmas) in London is a time of magic. The city is full of amazing lights, decorated trees and the sound of Christmas songs everywhere. Let's take a look at what things are happening during this wonderful time of year!**

Christmas carols

Carols are traditional Christmas songs that you can hear in the shops and on the streets of London. Groups of singers also give carol concerts at important London landmarks like in Trafalgar Square, St Paul's Cathedral, Westminster Abbey and Covent Garden.

Christmas carols in church

Pantomimes

Children in Britain often go to a pantomime at Christmas. Pantomimes are funny plays at the theatre. The stories are traditional and some popular pantomimes are Peter Pan, Cinderella, Sleeping Beauty, Jack and the Beanstalk and Snow White.

A traditional pantomime

Turn on the lights

Every year since 1947 Norway has given a Christmas tree to the people of London. The tree is transported by sea and then by road until it arrives in Trafalgar Square. It's covered with hundreds of white lights and they're usually turned on at the beginning of December. This is the start of Christmas time!

Let's go shopping!

London is also great for shopping during Christmas time. It's full of traditional Christmas markets and fairs selling Christmas food, handmade* presents, artwork and other Christmas things. The shops stay open until late and some give out free drinks and traditional Christmas sweets.

Events

In London during Christmas time, there are so many events to choose from. In Covent Garden there's the Great Christmas Pudding Race. In Greenwich Park there's the London Santa Run, with hundreds of people dressed as Santa running for charity. You can go ice skating on London's various ice rinks, visit Santa in his grotto and go for a winter swim in the Serpentine Lake in Hyde Park! Sound good?

handmade: made by hand, not by a machine

YUMMY THINGS TO EAT

26 After visiting all the things to see in the city, you're probably feeling a bit hungry! What would you like to eat? There are so many different kinds of food that you can find in London so let's try a few!

Food stalls*

While walking around the many markets in London, you'll probably see one of the yummy food stalls selling things that'll make you feel hungry. Jacket potatoes (whole potatoes cooked in their skin in the oven) with many different things inside, pies and pasties* with meat, vegetables and other things inside, hot soups and fish and chips.

A jacket potato

Pie and mash shops

Traditional food from London is pie and mash – a beef pie served with mashed potato' (see picture). It was the traditional working-class food in the East End of London and people sold it from carts* in the street. In 1890, a man called Albert Goddard opened the first pie and mash shop in the city, and there are about 80 of these shops still in London.

Pie and mash

Try some of our food!

Ethnic food

London is also famous for its large number of ethnic restaurants and whatever you want, you'll find it in London. There are Sushi bars, Chinese, Thai, Italian, Greek, Indian, French, Vietnamese, Brazilian restaurants and lots more. You can check where to go on *London Ethnic Eating*, a blog about ethnic food in London.

An e-table

Serve yourself

In the Soho area of London, there's a very unusual restaurant. You sit at an 'e-table', which has an interactive ordering system. Customers choose what they want to eat from a menu that is projected onto their table. They can also choose a virtual tablecloth and watch the chefs making the food through a web cam!

Do you want a jellied eel?

Jellied eels*

Another traditional working class food from the East End of London is Jellied eels. They're pieces of eel boiled in water and they are eaten hot or cold. You can find them together with pie and mash in shops called 'eel pie and mash' shops.

carts: wooden vehicles usually pulled by horses
stalls: a large table used for selling things
pasties: similar to pies, filled with meat or vegetables
eels: a long thin fish that is similar to a snake

LONDON ZOO

▶ 27 **If you would like to see a few zebras, tigers, monkeys and lots of other animals, then you can go to London Zoo for a fun day. Read on to find out more!**

London Zoo

London Zoo, also known as Regent's Zoo, is the world's oldest scientific zoo. It was opened in 1828 and it was used as a place for scientific study. In 1847, it was opened for people to visit. It now has more than 755 different kinds of animals and it's one of the biggest zoos in the UK.

Different animals

The zoo is home to about 16,800 animals and once a year the zookeepers count the number of animals. There are four different types of animal – mammals, birds, invertebrates and reptiles.

The zoo's most famous animal

One of the zoo's most popular animals was Guy the Gorilla. He arrived at the zoo in 1947 as a small baby and lived there until he died in 1978. He was a very gentle* animal and visitors to the zoo loved him. You can find a model of him at the Natural History Museum.

Unusual events

The zoo has different events during the year and one of the most popular is the late openings where people can visit the zoo at night. They have a 'silent disco' for teenagers, where they can visit the zoo with headphones while listening to music and see where and how the animals live at night.

Do you want to hold it?

Would you like to be a zookeeper?

If you like looking after animals, then why not be a zookeeper for a day? The zoo gives you a zookeeper's uniform which you can keep and you learn how to give food to the animals, clean them and the place where they sleep, and do other jobs that you have to do in a zoo.

The Human Zoo

A few years ago, the zoo had an event called the Human Zoo. 8 people were 'put on display*' and the idea was to show the basic nature of man as an animal and to look at the impact humans have on the animal kingdom.

gentle: kind and calm
display: show

ART

Where can you find an unusual art gallery in London? Unscramble the anagrams below!

1 TREMYCE C......................

2 TOMRALFP P......................

3 TRYPC C......................

4 LOITTE T......................

5 ARC KRAP C...................... P......................

BUILDINGS

Match the names of the buildings with their descriptions.

1 ☐ The Shard

2 ☐ The Gherkin

3 ☐ 23/24 Leinster Gardens

4 ☐ The smallest house in London

a It was sold for £630 million.

b Only one person has ever lived there.

c It isn't a real house.

d It was designed by an Italian architect.

THE CITY

Decide if each sentence is correct. Put A if it is correct, B if it is incorrect.

		A	B
1	The City's nickname is the Square Kilometre.	☐	☐
2	The City is an important financial centre.	☐	☐
3	Two important events take place in the City each year – the City of London Festival and the Lord Mayor's Show.	☐	☐
4	The Lord Mayor goes through the streets on a horse.	☐	☐
5	The City is a new area of London.	☐	☐

THE LONDON DUNGEONS

Imagine you are on a school trip at the London Dungeons. Send a postcard to your family telling them about what you're doing and what you can see there. Write about 50 words.

EVENTS

Can you match each event with where and when it takes place?

Event	**Where**	**When**
- Dino Snores	- Trafalgar Square	- April
- Carnival	- National History Museum	- December
- Underage Festival	- Victoria Park	- Once a month
- Pillow Fight	- Covent Garden	- August
- Great Christmas Pudding Race	- Notting Hill	- August

FILMS ABOUT LONDON

Be a film director! With your classmates think of an idea for a new film about London!
Choose the place where your film is set, the people in the film, the story and how much money you have to spend for the film, then present your idea to the class. Who has the best idea?

GREENWICH

Can you answer the questions about Greenwich?

1 What does GMT stand for?

2 Which line is Greenwich on?

3 What's the Palace of Placentia?

4 What's Greenwich's connection with the sea?

5 Why is Nauticalia the first shop in the world?

HARRODS

Can you find ten words in the wordsearch about Harrods? The words go down or across.

E	S	C	A	L	A	T	O	R	M
L	E	L	X	T	N	A	W	T	M
E	F	O	O	D	I	T	N	E	E
G	I	T	Y	S	M	B	E	C	M
A	M	H	U	P	A	N	R	M	O
N	N	E	G	U	L	I	M	U	R
T	I	S	D	E	S	F	R	P	I
T	V	O	C	C	W	I	O	P	A
R	G	R	O	C	E	R	Y	O	L
X	A	U	M	M	A	E	A	V	S
I	U	N	T	X	P	O	L	A	H

ICONS

▶ 10 **Listen to the text about London icons and put true or false.**

		T	F
1	Red double-decker buses were first used in 1966.	☐	☐
2	The red phone box has always had the same design.	☐	☐
3	It was possible to buy one of the 80 different phone boxes designed in 2012.	☐	☐
4	In London all taxis are black.	☐	☐
5	It's easy to become a taxi driver in London.	☐	☐
6	Beefeaters are a new attraction in the Tower of London.	☐	☐

THE CROWN JEWELS

Can you match the pictures of the royal objects with their name?

a crown	an orb	a ring	a sceptre	a sword	a spur

1 .... **2** .... **3** .... **4** .... **5** .... **6** ....

KIDSWEEK

Read the summary of Kidsweek and fill in the gaps with the missing word.

Kidsweek takes **(1)** .... every summer in London's **(2)** .... district, the West End. It **(3)** .... children up to the age of 16 the opportunity to **(4)** .... lots of theatre shows **(5)** .... free and take **(6)** .... in fun workshops **(7)** .... the stars.

LANDMARKS

Talk together with your classmates and answer the following questions.

Have you ever been to London?

- If yes, what did you see in London?
- What did you like best?
- Describe one of the landmarks you saw in London but don't say the name. Your partner has to guess!

- If no, look at the page about London landmarks.
- Which landmark would you like to visit?
- Describe one of the landmarks to your partner but don't say the name. Your partner has to guess!

MUSEUMS

Last week you visited one of the museums on pages 30-31. Write a message to your friend telling him/her what you did there, what you liked and didn't like about it.

NATURE

In May 2013 London's first ever Tree Week began. What can you do to make your city greener? Make a list and then see what your classmates have written.

OUTSIDE LONDON

Can you divide the snake into the four different places to visit outside London that you read about on pages 34-35?
How many different words can you make out of the snake?
Eg. Food, phone... Make at least 20!

windsorcastlegoapehamptoncourtpalacechessingtonworldofadventure

PEOPLE

Match the words to the pictures.

Pearly Kings and Queens
Commuters
A tourist

1 ....

2 ....

3 ....

THE QUEEN

Listen to the text about Queen Elizabeth.

18 **1** What are the Queen's two middle names?

2 How many children does she have?

3 What does she usually do on a normal day?

4 How many birthdays does she have?

RECREATION

Look at the definitions and complete the missing words.

1 A place where you can find things to buy at a good price.
_ _ _ _ _ _ _ _

2 If you want to sell your things at one of these you have to get up very early. _ _ _ _   _ _ _ _ _ _   _ _ _ _ _ _

3 One of the most famous green areas. _ _ _ _ _ _   _ _ _ _ _ _

4 A Victorian public toilet, a bicycle repair shop and a crypt are all examples of this. _ _ _ _ _ _ _ _ _ _   _ _ _ _ _ _

Test your memory

Can you remember what you read on the pages from 42 to 57? Test yourself by answering the questions in two minutes. Ready, steady, go!

1 Name 4 sports that are popular in London.

2 Where can you say what you think in London?

3 Where can you drink 17 different types of tea in London?

4 What's used by 3.5 million people every day in London?

5 What happens on No Trousers Day in London?

6 What different 'vehicles' can you use to get around London?

7 Name four modern writers from London.

8 Name the different things you can do during Christmas time.

9 If you're feeling hungry, what can you eat in London?

10 Who was Guy the Gorilla?

Syllabus

Topics
Art - Nature - Museums - Sport - Culture and traditions - Food - People - Transport

Notions and concepts
Describing places - Describing events - Talking about traditions - Describing different means of transport - Making suggestions - Likes and dislikes - Making an itinerary - Describing typical things to eat

Other
Adverbs - Adjectives - Prepositions - Comparatives and superlatives - Present simple - Past simple - Present perfect - Gerunds